中华人民共和国文化和旅游部
2017 年文化发展统计公报

STATISTICAL COMMUNIQUÉ OF THE MINISTRY OF CULTURE AND TOURISM OF THE PEOPLE'S REPUBLIC OF CHINA ON CULTURAL DEVELOPMENT IN 2017

中华人民共和国文化和旅游部 编

中国统计出版社
China Statistics Press

图书在版编目（CIP）数据

中华人民共和国文化和旅游部2017年文化发展统计公报 / 中华人民共和国文化和旅游部编 . -- 北京 : 中国统计出版社 , 2018.5
ISBN 978-7-5037-8465-1

Ⅰ . ①中… Ⅱ . ①中… Ⅲ . ①文化发展－统计分析－研究报告－中国－2017 Ⅳ . ① G12

中国版本图书馆CIP数据核字(2018)第082884号

中华人民共和国文化和旅游部2017年文化发展统计公报

作　　者 / 中华人民共和国文化和旅游部
责任编辑 / 李　冲
装帧设计 / 黄　晨
出版发行 / 中国统计出版社
通信地址 / 北京市西城区月坛南街57号
邮政编码 / 100826
办公地址 / 北京市丰台区西三环南路甲6号
网　　址 / http://www.zgtjcbs.com
电　　话 /（010）63376907（发行部）
印　　刷 / 北京画中画印刷有限公司
经　　销 / 新华书店
廾　　本 / 880×1230毫米　1/16
字　　数 / 50千字
印　　张 / 2.5
版　　别 / 2018年5月第1版
版　　次 / 2018年5月北京第1次印刷
定　　价 / 28.00元

目录

CONTENTS

中华人民共和国文化和旅游部 2017 年文化发展统计公报 [1]

2017 年，全国文化系统以习近平新时代中国特色社会主义思想为指导，全面落实党的十八大和十八届三中、四中、五中、六中、七中全会精神，深入学习贯彻党的十九大精神，紧紧围绕“五位一体”总体布局和“四个全面”战略布局，坚持中国特色社会主义文化发展道路，坚定文化自信，坚守中华文化立场，坚持以人民为中心的工作导向，以高度的政治责任感和历史使命感，推动社会主义核心价值观和中华优秀传统文化广泛弘扬，公共文化服务水平不断提高，艺术创作持续繁荣，文化市场规范有序，文化产业蓬勃发展，国家文化软实力和中华文化影响力大幅提升，社会主义文化强国建设迈出了坚实步伐。

一、机构和人员

2017 年末，纳入统计范围的全国各类文化（文物）单位 [2] 32.64 万个，比上年末增加 1.58 万个；

图 1　2006 年 –2017 年全国文化单位机构数及从业人员数

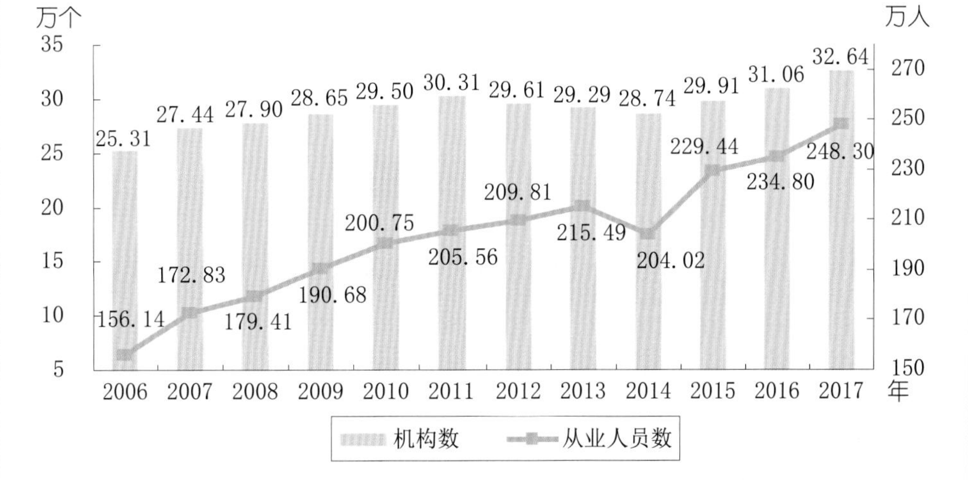

从业人员[3]248.30 万人，增加 13.50 万人。其中，各级文化文物部门所属单位 66738 个，增加 709 个；从业人员 66.72 万人，增加 0.64 万人。

二、艺术创作演出

2017 年，全国艺术院团继续开展“深入生活、扎根人民”主题实践活动，深入贯彻落实习近平总书记在文艺工作座谈会、在中国文联十大和中国作协九大开幕式上的重要讲话以及给乌兰牧骑队员们的回信精神，坚持以人民为中心的创作导向，树立精品意识，攀登艺术高峰。中央直属院团共开展蹲点创作、体验生活、服务基层、结对帮扶活动 500 余项，开展公益性演出 1200 余场，新建基层联系点 12 个，2017 年元旦和春节期间组织 44 支文艺小分队赴基层开展慰问演出、文化服务等惠民活动。实施戏曲振兴工程，完成全国地方戏曲剧种普查，基本掌握全国 348 个戏曲剧种基础数据。持续发挥重大工程项目的导向和示范作用，深入实施国家舞台艺术精品创作扶持工程、中国民族音乐舞蹈杂技扶持发展工程、中国民族歌剧传承发展工程、国家美术发展和收藏工程、剧本扶持工程。精心组织开展 2017 年国家艺术院团演出季、全国基层院团戏曲会演、2017 年全国美术馆馆藏精品展出季、“文华奖”获奖剧目全国巡演、全国曲艺木偶剧皮影戏优秀剧目展演、全国小剧场戏剧优秀剧目展演、第二届中国民族器乐民间乐种组合展演、第八届中国京剧艺术节、第三届中国歌剧节、第四届中国西部交响乐周、第五届中国诗歌节、潘天寿诞辰 120 周年系列纪念活动、中国话剧诞生

表 1　2007 年 –2017 年全国艺术表演团体基本情况

年　份	机构数（个）	从业人员数（人）	演出场次（万场）	国内演出观众人次（万人次）	总收入（万元）	
						# 演出收入
2007 年	4512	220653	92.7	75895.6	829045	203757
2008 年	5114	208174	90.5	63186.8	933685	204842
2009 年	6139	184678	120.2	81715.9	1121559	288214
2010 年	6864	185413	137.1	88455.8	1239255	342696
2011 年	7055	226599	154.7	74585.1	1540263	526745
2012 年	7321	242047	135.0	82805.1	1968802	641480
2013 年	8180	260865	165.1	90064.3	2800266	820738
2014 年	8769	262887	173.9	91019.7	2264046	757028
2015 年	10787	301840	210.8	95799.0	2576483	939313
2016 年	12301	332920	230.6	118137.7	3112276	1308591
2017 年	15752	403197	293.8	124862.9	3421091	1478239

110 周年纪念座谈会等重大艺术活动，集中展示优秀艺术成果。对艺术创作的资金扶持力度进一步加大，国家艺术基金 2017 年共立项资助项目 1001 项，资助金额 7.38 亿元。

年末全国共有艺术表演团体[4]15752 个，比上年末增加 3451 个，从业人员 40.32 万人，增加 7.03 万人。其中各级文化部门所属的艺术表演团体 2074 个，占 13.2%，从业人员 11.56 万人，占 28.7%。

全年全国艺术表演团体共演出 293.77 万场，比上年增长 27.4%，其中赴农村演出 184.44 万场，增长 21.7%，赴农村演出场次占总演出场次的 62.8%；国内观众 12.49 亿人次，比上年增长 5.7%，其中农村观众 8.30 亿人次，增长 33.8%；总收入 342.11 亿元，比上年增长 9.9%，其中演出收入 147.82 亿元，增长 13.0%。

全年全国艺术表演团体共组织政府采购公益演出 16.07 万场，观众 1.32 亿人次，分别比上年增长 12.9% 和 10.2%。利用流动舞台车演出 11.80 万场次，观众 1.02 亿人次。

年末全国共有艺术表演场馆 2455 个，比上年末增加 170 个。观众坐席数 179.61 万个，比上年增长 6.3%。其中各级文化部门所属艺术表演场馆 1253 个，全年共举行艺术演出 7.10 万场次，增长 4.3%；艺术演出观众人次 2713 万人次，增长 4.8%；艺术演出收入 6.92 亿元，增长 25.0%。

年末全国美术馆 499 个，比上年末增加 36 个，从业人员 4576 人，减少 21 人。全年共举办展览 6757 次，比上年增长 9.9%，参观人次 3724 万人次，增长 15.0%。

三、公共文化服务体系

2017 年，进一步贯彻落实《关于加快构建现代公共文化服务体系的意见》和国家基本公共文化服务指导标准，积极推动出台《中华人民共和国公共图书馆法》，部署开展《公共文化服务保障法》暨中央重点改革任务落实情况督查工作，切实推动法律和各项改革措施落地生根。召开公共文化服务效能建设现场经验交流会，推广“文化服务云”“百姓文化超市”等典型经验。开展乡镇综合文化站服务效能抽查工作，督促各地整改问题，进一步提升服务水平。推进数字文化馆、数字图书馆及移动阅读平台建设，创新数字化服务模式。推动公共文化服务社会化，探索开展公共文化设施社会化运营试点。

（一）公共图书馆[5]

年末全国共有公共图书馆 3166 个，比上年末增加 13 个。年末全国公共图书馆从业人员 57567 人，比上年末增加 359 人。其中具有高级职称的人员 6502 人，占 11.3%；具有中级职称的人员 18729 人，占 32.5%。

年末全国公共图书馆实际使用房屋建筑面积 1515.27 万平方米，比上年末增长 6.4%；图书总藏量[6]96953 万册，增长 7.5%，其中古籍 2701 万册，与上年基本持平；电子图书[7]102627 万册，增长 15.6%；阅览室坐席数 106.42 万个，增长 7.9%；计算机 22.10 万台，增长 4.4%，其中供读者使用的电子阅览终端 14.43 万台，增长 7.0 %。

年末全国平均每万人公共图书馆建筑面积 109.0 平方米，比上年末增加 6.0 平方米；全国人均图书藏量 0.70 册，增加 0.05 册；全年全国人均购书费 1.70 元，比上年增加 0.14 元。

图 2　2006 年 –2017 年全国公共图书馆人均资源情况

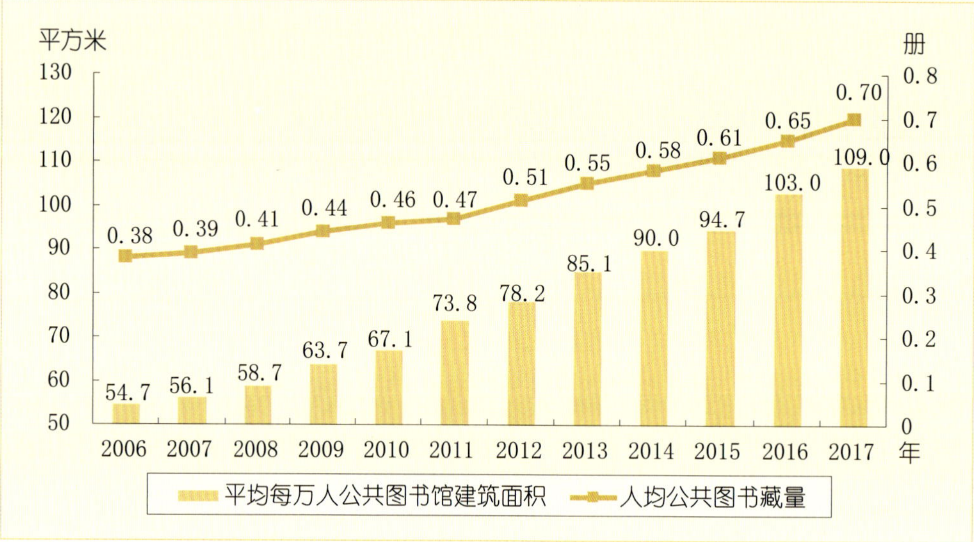

全年全国公共图书馆发放借书证[8]6736 万个，比上年增长 20.4%；总流通人次[9]74450 万，增长 12.7%。书刊文献外借册次 55091 万，增长 0.7%；外借人次 25503 万，增长 2.5%。全年共为读者举办各种活动 155590 次，增长 11.1%；参加人次 8857 万，增长 24.1%。

图 3　2006 年 –2017 年全国公共图书馆总流通人次及书刊外借册次

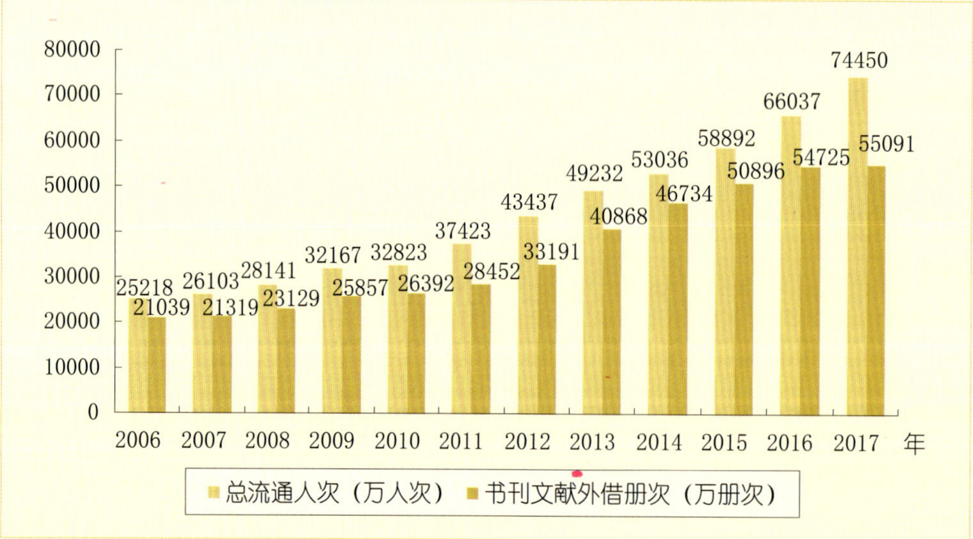

（二）群众文化机构[10]

年末全国共有群众文化机构 44521 个，比上年末增加 24 个。其中乡镇综合文化站 33997 个，比上年末减少 243 个。年末全国群众文化机构从业人员 180911 人，比上年末减少 1119 人。其中具有高级职称的人员 6171 人，占 3.4%；具有中级职称的人员 17224 人，占 9.5%。

年末全国群众文化机构实际使用房屋建筑面积 4106.85 万平方米，比上年末增长 2.9%；业务用房面积 2977.46 万平方米，增长 2.7%。年末全国平均每万人群众文化设施建筑面积 295.44 平方米，比上年末提高 6.80 平方米。

图 4　2006 年 –2017 年全国平均每万人群众文化设施建筑面积

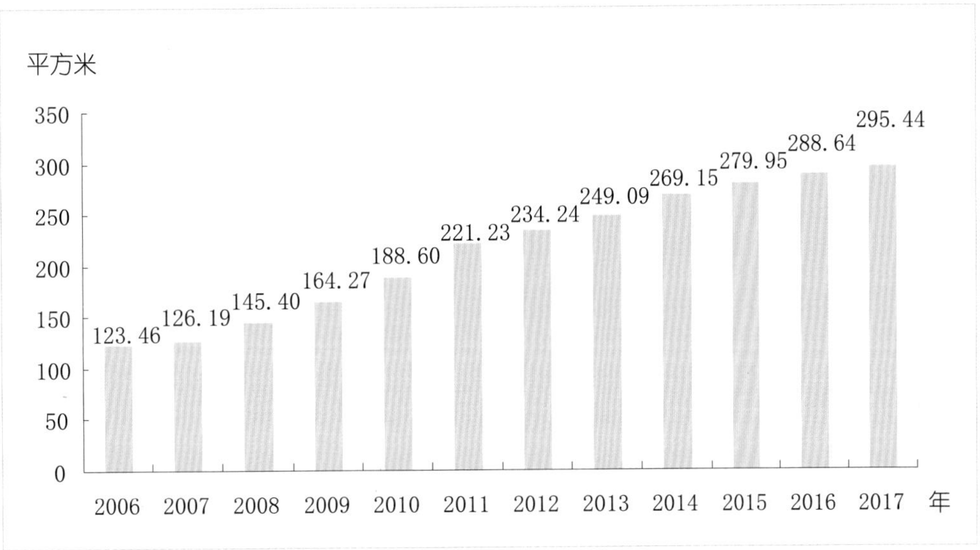

全年全国群众文化机构共组织开展各类文化活动[11]197.86 万场次，比上年增长 7.6%；服务人次 63951 万，增长 10.5%。

表 2　2017 年全国群众文化机构开展活动情况

项　目	总量		比上年增长（%）	
	活动次数（万次）	服务人次（万人次）	活动次数	服务人次
各项活动总计	197.86	63951	7.6	10.5
其中：展览	15.41	10711	2.7	-0.7
文艺活动	111.43	48183	4.6	13.8
公益性讲座	3.44	562	1.8	7.7
训练班	67.59	4494	14.5	5.7

年末全国群众文化机构共有馆办文艺团体[12]8241 个，演出 15.82 万场，观众 8229 万人次。由文化馆（站）指导的群众业余文艺团体 41.67 万个，馆办老年大学 865 个。

四、文化市场

2017 年，进一步实施源头治理，支持引导文化市场经营单位改进服务、转变形象，促进行业健康发展、市场规范有序。确定 99 个示范地区、649 家示范场所，实施阳光娱乐行动计划，支持开展“阳光娱乐”品牌活动，扩大文化消费。印发《关于引导迷你歌咏亭市场健康发展的通知》，将全国 5.4 万个迷你歌咏亭纳入备案管理。修订《娱乐场所管理办法》，研究制订《关于对文化市场领域严重违法失信市场主体及有关人员开展联合惩戒的合作备忘录》，开展“放管服”政策落实和行政审批规范化督查，打通政策落地“最后一公里”。深化文化市场综合执法改革，推进文化市场综合执法队伍建设，实施中西部地区文化市场综合执法能力提升（2017–2020）行动计划。开展“双随机一公开”执法检查，组织查办 190 件文化市场重大案件，检查 100 家主要网络表演经营单位，排查手机直播应用软件 11386 款，下线 3653 款手机表演平台软件。

年末全国文化市场经营单位[13]25.74 万家，比上年末增加 1.47 万家；从业人员 173.37 万人，增加 12.42 万人。年末全国共有娱乐场所 78616 个，从业人员 60.01 万人，全年营业总收入 546.87 亿元，增长 1.5%，营业利润 130.69 亿元，增长 3.9%；互联网上网服务营业场所 143434 个，从业人员 44.09 万人，全年营业总收入 382.59 亿元，降低 11.5%，营业利润 107.18 亿元，降低 18.4%。

五、文化产业与文化科技

2017 年，加强文化产业发展顶层设计，出台了一系列促进文化产业发展的政策文件。《文化产业促进法》起草工作稳步推进并形成了征求意见稿。制定出台《文化部“十三五”时期文化产业发展规划》，明确“十三五”时期文化产业发展总体要求、主要任务、重点行业和保障措施，为全国文化产业创新发展提供指引。推动出台《国务院办公厅关于进一步激发社会领域投资活力的意见》，首次明确提出推进文化等领域“投贷联动”。推动出台《社会领域产业专项债券发行指引》，推出文化产业专项债券。印发《关于推动数字文化产业创新发展的指导意见》，成为国家层面首个针对数字文化产业的宏观性、指导性政策文件。

制定出台《中国文化艺术政府奖动漫奖评奖办法》，组织开展第三届动漫奖评奖工作。制定《动漫游戏产业“一带一路”国际合作行动计划》，发挥动漫游戏产业在文化产业国际合作中的先导作用。年末经原文化部、财政部、国家税务总局三部门联合认定的动漫企业共有 730 个，重点动漫企业 43 个。

推进文化产业园区创建发展和规范管理，研究创建验收管理指标体系，公布第一批获得国家级文化产业示范园区创建资格的 10 家园区名单，完成对现有国家级文化产业园区的专项清理检查。年末全国共有 1 个国家文化产业创新实验区，1 个国家动漫产业园，10 个国家级文化产业示范园区，10 个国家级文化产业试验园区和 335 个国家文化产业示范基地。

公布第一批第二次 19 个国家文化消费试点城市名单，指导试点城市明确工作方向、创新试点模式，开展实地督察、专项督察，督促试点城市加快推进工作。截止 2017 年底，45 个试点城市累计参与人次超过 3 亿，拉动文化消费规模超过 900 亿元。推动文化文物单位文创产品开发，通过中央财政文化产业发展专项资金等渠道加大支持和指导力度，2017 年 154 家试点单位文创产品全年经营收入近 15 亿元，同比增长 20%。

进一步完善《文化与金融合作示范区创建工作方案》，确定北京市东城区、浙江省宁波市为首批国家文化与金融合作示范区创建候选地区，深化文化金融合作。组织开展 2017 年度中央财政文化产业发展专项资金重大项目征集遴选工作，共推荐 446 个申报项目，金额共计 5.88 亿元。开展第四批 PPP 示范项目申报工作，推动 450 个文化基础设施项目和 624 个文化旅游项目纳入财政部 PPP 综合信息平台，投资额共计 8287 亿元。

根据国家统计局统计，2017 年全国 5.5 万家规模以上文化及相关产业企业实现营业收入 91950 亿元，比上年增长 10.8%，增速提高 3.3 个百分点，持续保持较快增长。

2017 年，制定出台《文化部“十三五”时期文化科技创新规划》，明确提出了建设文化科技创新体系的基本思路、主要任务、重点工程和保障措施。全国艺术科学规划项目资助体系进一步完善，2017 年立项总数达 336 项，资助总额超过 6800 万元，发挥了全国艺术科学规划项目引领作用。加强国家科技支撑计划、国家文化创新工程等科研项目管理，12 个国家文化创新工程项目获得立项。深化文化标准化改革，文化领域标准清单及国家标准文本全部向社会公开。实施文化智库体系建设工程，设立文化智库项目 14 个，指导成立“全国省级艺术研究院（所）联盟”，推动艺术研究机构更好地发挥智库作用，在腾讯、百度、阿里巴巴等 5 家企业设立首批文化智库企业联系点。

六、文化遗产保护

2017 年，坚决贯彻习近平总书记关于文物工作的重要指示精神，深入落实国务院《关于进一步加强文物工作的指导意见》，扎实推进文物保护各项重点工作。编制长城保护总体规划，基本完成省级长城保护规划编制工作，开展长城执法专项督察“回头看”。开展“考古中国”重大研究，推进大遗址保护，公布第三批 12 家国家考古遗址公园名单。编制革命文物保护传承五年行动计划，启动“长征－红色记忆”工程，编制《长征文化遗产线路总体规划》，推进延安革命遗址、赣南等原中央苏区旧址等项目实施。“鼓浪屿：历史国际社区”成功入选《世界遗产名录》，截至目前中国共有 52 项世界遗产，总数位列世界第二。全面完成第一次全国可移动文物普查，共普查全国可移动文物 1.08 亿件（套）、文物收藏单位 1.1 万余个，基本摸清国有可移动文物家底。年末全国不可移动文物共有 76.67 万件。修订完善国家一二三级博物馆运行评估规则和指标，印发《关于进一步推动非国有博物馆发展的意见》，启动国有馆藏一级文物复核和非国有博物馆藏品备案。全面实施“互联网＋中华文明”三年行动计划，推进文物信息资源开放共享。

年末全国共有各类文物机构 9931 个，比上年末增加 977 个。其中，文物保护管理机构 3518 个，占 35.4%，博物馆[14]4721 个，占 47.5%。年末全国文物机构从业人员 16.16 万人，比上年末增加 1.01 万人。其中高级职称 9221 人，占 5.7%，中级职称 20136 人，占 12.5%。

图 5　2006 年 –2017 年全国文物机构及从业人员情况

年末全国文物机构拥有文物藏品 5096.32 万件，比上年末增加 640.44 万件 / 套，增长 14.4%。其中，博物馆文物藏品 3938.32 万件 / 套，占文物藏品总量的 77.3%；文物商店文物藏品 739.18 万件 / 套，占 14.5%。

2017 年全国各类文物机构共举办陈列展览 26045 个，比上年增加 1424 个。其中，基本陈列[15]13025 个，比上年增加 823 个；临时展览[16]13020 个，比上年增加 601 个。接待观众 114773 万人次，比上年增长 13.3%，其中未成年人 28909 万人次，增长 9.9%，占参观总人数的 25.2%。博物馆接待观众 97172 万人次，增长 14.2%，占文物机构接待观众总数的 84.7%。

2017 年，积极会同有关部门，制定印发《中国传统工艺振兴计划》，全面部署传统工艺振兴工作。研究制定第一批国家传统工艺振兴目录，支持设立 10 个传统工艺工作站，提升传统工艺发展水平，助力精准扶贫；支持 19 个省（区、市）开展 28 项非遗传承人对话系列活动，推动传承人与设计、研究机构开展项目合作，促进传统工艺融入当代生活。指导 78 所高校实施 2017 年度非遗传承人群研修研习培训计划，举办研培班 196 期。启用研培计划信息管理平台，设立咨询专家库，举办师资

图 6　2008 年 –2017 年全国文物机构接待观众人次及未成年人观众人次

培训班和经验交流会，促进参与高校加强对非遗保护和研培工作的理论研究。举办传统戏剧、民俗、老字号非遗项目研培班，进一步扩展了研培计划覆盖门类和参与范围。

对 839 名国家级非遗代表性传承人开展抢救性记录，对 2015 年支持的 268 名国家级非遗代表性传承人抢救性记录项目开展通查和验收。年末共有国家级非物质文化遗产代表性传承人 1986 人，国家级非物质文化遗产代表性项目 1372 项。进一步加强国家级非物质文化遗产保护利用设施建设，安排中央预算内投资 3.35 亿元支持建设 46 个国家级非遗保护利用设施，有效推动了非物质文化遗产保护传承与经济社会发展的有机结合。

开展 2017 年文化和自然遗产日活动，全国共举办 2000 多项大中型非遗宣传展示活动，线上线下观众超过 1 亿人次。以传承发展的生动实践为主题，办好第六届中国成都国际非物质文化遗产节，将 579 场生动多样的演出活动送进 326 个基层社区。年末全国共有非物质文化遗产保护机构 2466 个，从业人员 17235 人。全年全国各类非物质文化遗产保护机构举办演出 50178 场，增长 19.0%，观众 4558 万人次，增长 16.8%；举办民俗活动 15133 次，增长 3.9%，观众 6211 万人次，增长 34.5%。

七、对外和对港澳台文化交流

2017 年，积极推动文化外交活动机制化，深度参与中俄、中美、中欧等八大高级别人文交流机制。截至 2017 年底，我国已与 157 个国家签署了文化合作协定，累计签署文化交流执行计划近 800 个，初步形成了覆盖世界主要国家和地区的政府间文化交流与合作网络。主办“中美文化论坛”、第十五届亚洲艺术节、“东亚文化之都”、“欧洲文化之都”合作论坛、首届金砖国家文化节、第三届中国 – 中东欧国家文化合作部长论坛和“意会中国”“中非文化聚焦”等文化交流活动，进一步扩大中华文化国际影响力。

建立“一带一路”文化交流机制，夯实互联互通基础，建立健全丝绸之路国际剧院、博物馆、艺术节、图书馆、美术馆联盟。举办第四届“丝绸之路国际艺术节”、第三届“海上丝绸之路国际艺术节”和第二届丝绸之路（敦煌）国际文化博览会，参展参演国家和地区总数、演出场次、参展艺术品数量、成交额等再创新高。开展“一带一路”文化贸易与投资重点项目征集活动，培育一批重点文化企业和文化项目，进一步推进与“一带一路”沿线国家文化贸易发展。

以讲好中国故事为主线，2017 年“欢乐春节”在全球 140 多个国家和地区的 500 余座城市举办了 2000 多项文化活动，“欢乐春节”品牌效应逐步形成。海外中国文化中心建设顺利推进，2017 年希腊雅典文化中心、越南河内文化中心、保加利亚索非亚文化中心、以色列特拉维夫文化中心、缅甸仰光文化中心等 5 个海外中国文化中心揭牌或启用，海外中国文化中心总数达 35 个。

积极落实内地与港澳文化交流合作执行计划，持续打造“根与魂”“艺海流金”等品牌项目。对台文化交流与合作稳步推进，“情系中华—海峡两岸文化创意产业展”“守望精神家园—两岸非物质文化遗产月”等品牌活动反响热烈。

全年经文化系统审批的对外文化交流项目 3054 起，63961 人次参加；对港澳文化交流项目 496 项，12567 人次参加；对台文化交流项目 342 项，6428 人次参加。

八、文化资金投入

2017 年，中央财政通过继续实施“三馆一站”免费开放、非物质文化遗产保护、公共数字文化建设等文化项目，共落实中央补助地方专项资金 49.33 亿元，比上年降低 19.2%。

图 7　2006 年 –2017 年中央对地方文化项目补助资金情况

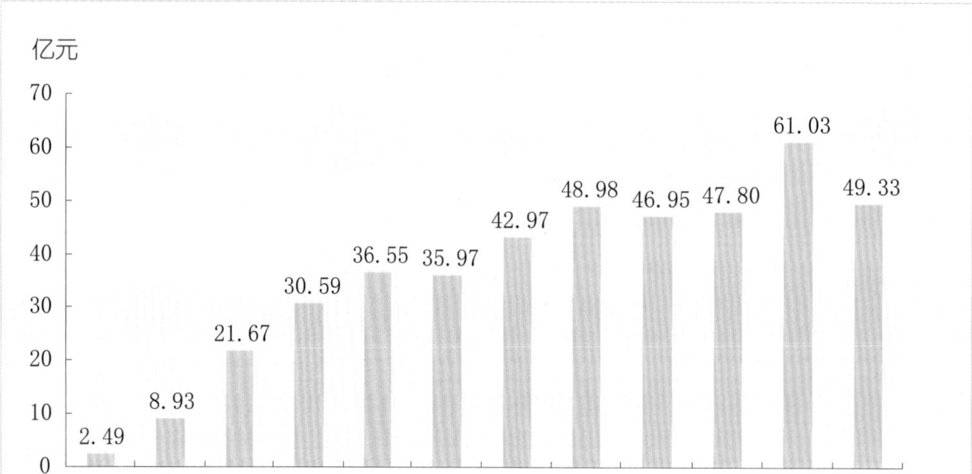

全年全国文化事业费[17]855.80 亿元，比上年增加 85.11 亿元，增长 11.0%；全国人均文化事业

费 61.57 元，比上年增加 5.83 元，增长 10.5%。

图 8　2006 年 -2017 年全国人均文化事业费及增速情况

文化事业费占财政总支出的比重为 0.42%，比重比上年提高 0.01 个百分点。

图 9　全国文化事业费占财政总支出比重

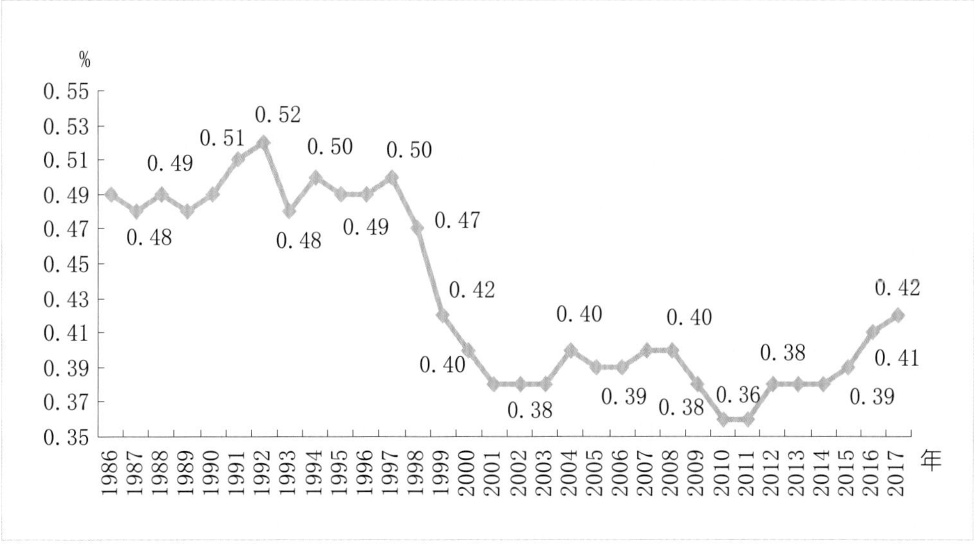

全国文化事业费中，县以上文化单位 398.35 亿元，占 46.5%，比重比上年降低了 1.6 个百分点；县及县以下文化单位 457.45 亿元，占 53.5%，比重比上年提高了 1.6 个百分点。东部地区 [18] 文化单位文化事业费 381.71 亿元，占 44.6%，比重提高了 1.3 个百分点；中部地区文化单位 213.30 亿元，占 24.9%，比重提高了 0.9 个百分点；西部地区文化单位 230.70 亿元，占 27.0%，比重下降了 1.3 个百分点。

表 3　全国文化事业费按城乡和区域分布情况

项　目		1995 年	2000 年	2005 年	2010 年	2015 年	2016 年	2017 年
总量（亿元）	全国	33.39	63.16	133.82	323.06	682.97	770.69	855.80
	#县以上	24.44	46.33	98.12	206.65	352.84	371.00	398.35
	县及县以下	8.95	16.87	35.70	116.41	330.13	399.68	457.45
	#东部地区	13.43	28.85	64.37	143.35	287.87	333.62	381.71
	中部地区	9.54	15.05	30.58	78.65	164.27	184.80	213.30
	西部地区	8.30	13.70	27.56	85.78	193.87	218.17	230.70
所占比重（%）	全国	100.0	100.0	100.0	100.0	100.0	100.0	100.0
	#县以上	73.2	73.4	73.3	64.0	51.7	48.1	46.5
	县及县以下	26.8	26.7	26.7	36.0	48.3	51.9	53.5
	#东部地区	40.2	45.7	48.1	44.4	42.1	43.3	44.6
	中部地区	28.6	23.8	22.9	24.3	24.1	24.0	24.9
	西部地区	24.9	21.7	20.6	26.6	28.4	28.3	27.0

全年全国文物事业费[19]355.59 亿元，比上年增加 47.89 亿元，增长 15.6%；文物事业费占财政总支出的比重为 0.17%，比重比上年提高 0.01 个百分点。

据财政部统计，2017 年全国财政支出中，文化体育传媒经费[20]3367 亿元，比上年增长 6.4%，占财政支出的 1.66%，比重比上年下降 0.02 个百分点。

图 10　2006 年 –2017 年全国文化体育传媒经费总量及增长速度

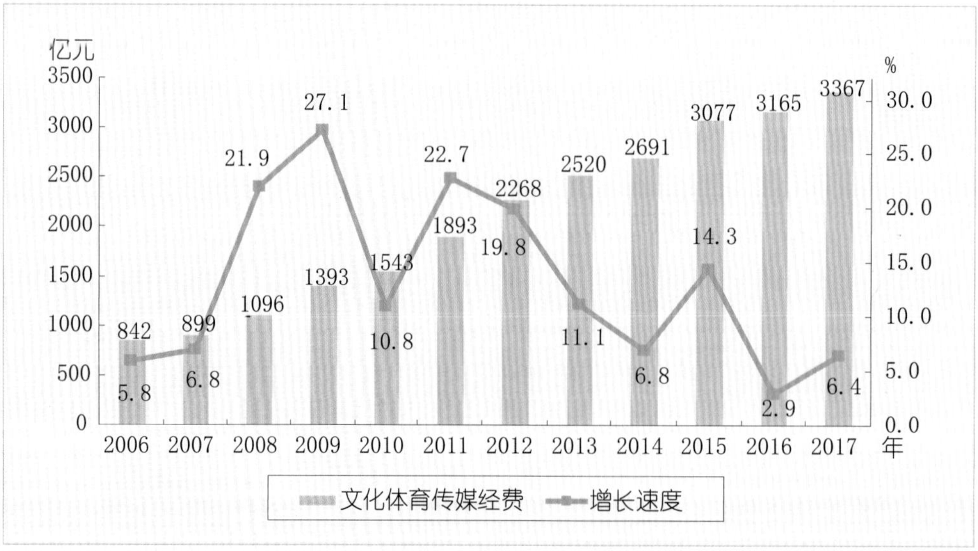

注释：

[1] 本公报中各项数据为初步统计数据。各项统计数据均未包括香港特别行政区、澳门特别行政区和台湾省。部分数据因四舍五入的原因，存在着与分项合计不等的情况。

[2] 文化单位是指全国各级文化部门（含文化系统和文物系统）主办的或实行行业管理的文化机构，不含各级新闻出版、广播影视等部门主办或管理的文化机构。根据现行的统计制度，文化部门主办的文化单位（如公共图书馆、文化馆、文化站、博物馆、公有制艺术表演团体、公有制艺术表演场馆等）全部纳入了统计范围，实行行业管理的文化单位中，娱乐场所和互联网上网服务营业场所、非公有制艺术表演团体、非公有制艺术表演场馆、经营性互联网文化单位、艺术品经营机构和演出经纪机构均纳入统计。

[3] 从业人员是指在各级文化部门（含文化系统和文物系统）主办或实行行业管理的机构中工作并取得劳动报酬的人员。统计范围同文化单位。

[4] 艺术表演团体指由文化部门主办或实行行业管理（经文化行政部门审批并领取营业性演出许可证），专门从事表演艺术等活动的各类专业艺术表演团体。

[5] 公共图书馆是指由各级文化部门主办的、面向社会公众开放并提供科学、文化等各种知识普及教育的机构。

[6] 公共图书馆总藏量指已编目的古籍、图书、期刊和报纸的合订本、手册、手稿，以及缩微制品、录像带、录音带、光盘等视听文献资料数量之和，不包括电子图书。

[7] 指通过购买方式取得当前使用权的电子图书，以及本馆自建或与其他机构合作建设的电子图书。

[8] 公共图书馆发放的借书证数是指由公共图书馆发放，并在当年内使用过至少一次的借书证数。

[9] 公共图书馆总流通人次是指本年度内到图书馆场馆接受图书馆服务的总人次，包括借阅书刊、咨询问题，以及参加各类读者活动等。

[10] 群众文化机构是指各级文化部门主办的开展群众文化活动的场所，主要包括文化馆（含综合性文化中心、群众艺术馆）、文化站。

[11] 群众文化机构组织开展活动是指组织文艺活动、举办训练班、举办展览和组织公益性讲座总和。

[12] 群众文化机构馆办文艺团体指由本馆人员组成的为群众提供文艺演出的演出团队。

[13] 文化市场经营单位指经文化市场行政部门审批或备案并领取相关许可或备案文件的、从事文化经营和文化服务活动的机构。按照现行统计制度，文化市场经营单位统计范围包括娱乐场所和互联网上网服务营业场所、非公有制艺术表演团体、非公有制艺术表演场馆、经营性互联网文化单位、

艺术品经营机构和演出经纪机构。

[14] 博物馆指为了研究、教育、欣赏的目的，收藏、保护、展示人类活动和自然环境的见证物，向公众开放，非营利性、永久性社会服务机构，包括以博物馆（院）、纪念馆（舍）、科技馆、陈列馆等专有名称开展活动的单位。

[15] 基本陈列指在本馆布置陈列、地点固定、时间较长的展出。

[16] 临时展览指在本机构内设置，由本馆设计布陈，形式比较多样的展出。

[17] 文化事业费是指区域内各级财政对文化系统主办单位的经费投入总和。根据现行统计口径，文化事业费不包括各级文化行政管理部门的行政运行经费。

[18] 东部地区包括北京、天津、辽宁、上海、江苏、浙江、福建、山东、广东；中部地区包括河北、山西、吉林、黑龙江、安徽、江西、河南、湖北、湖南、海南；西部地区包括内蒙古、广西、重庆、四川、贵州、云南、西藏、陕西、甘肃、青海、宁夏、新疆。

[19] 文物事业费是指区域内各级财政对文物事业的经费投入总和。一般包括博物馆、文物保护管理机构等文物事业单位的财政拨款（不含基建拨款）及文物部门所属企业的财政补贴。

[20] 文化体育传媒经费数据源自财政部，是指各级政府在文化、文物、体育、广播影视和新闻出版方面的投入。

Statistical Communiqué of the Ministry of Culture and Tourism of the People's Republic of China on Cultural Development in 2017[1]

In 2017, under the guidance of the Thought on Socialism with Chinese characteristics for the new era put forward by President Xi Jinping, all official cultural departments in China have implemented and put into practice the the guiding principles from the 18th CPC National Congress, the 3rd, 4th, 5th, 6th and 7th Plenary Session of the 18th CPC Central Committee and the 19th CPC National Congress, and worked in accordance with the "Five-Pronged Overall Plan" and "Four Comprehensives" strategy to promote all-round economic, political, cultural, social, and ecological progress in China.With the aim to further promote socialist culture with Chinese characteristics and consolidate confidence in culture as their historic mission, they put people at the center of their work with high sense of responsibility, disseminated socialist core values and the best of time-honored Chinese culture, upgraded public cultural services, encouraged vibrant cultural and creative productions and a regulated, orderly cultural market, and promoted the growth of cultural industries. Their work facilitated steady strides in the cause of building a culturally strong socialist China.

I. Institution and Employment

326,400 national cultural units[2] were brought into the statistical range by the end of 2017, 15,800 more than that of the previous year end; the number of employees[3] was 2.483 million, 135 thousand persons more than the previous year. Among them, 66,738 units were affiliated to government cultural departments, 709 more than those of the past year, with 667,200 employees, 6,400 persons more than those of the previous year.

Figure 1: Number of national cultural units and employed persons in 2006-2017

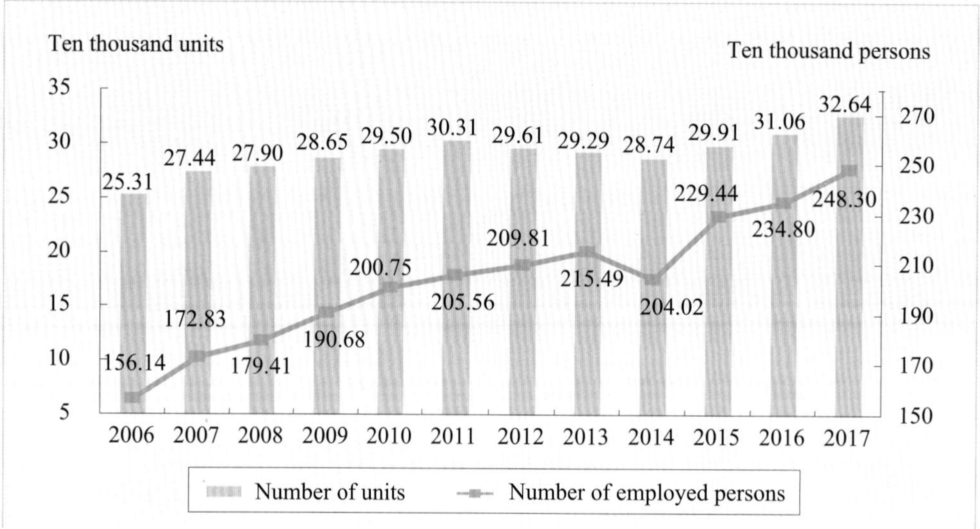

II. Performing Arts

In 2017, performing art troupes all across China continued to put the spirit of "drawing inspiration from real life and the people" and Secretary General Xi Jinping's speeches on the forum of cultural and art professionals, the opening ceremonies of the 10th Conference of China Federation of Literary and Art Circles and the 9th Conference of China Writers' Association, and his letter to Ulanmuqi artists into practice, put people at the center of their work, and endeavored to reach artistic excellence. Performing arts troupes under direct administration of the central government have conducted more than 500 programs to deliver arts to the grassroot communities on a hands-on and point-to-point base, given more than 1200 nonn-profit shows, built 12 new contact hubs in grassroot communities, and sent 44 artists teams to visit communities during the 2017 new year's time and Chinese new year's time. The Chinese traditional opera revitalization project was implemented based on the census of all local operas in China, which yielded basic date for 348 opera schools nationwide. The projects to foster excellent national performing arts productions, support Chinese traditional music, dance and acrobatics, promote national operas, foster fine arts growth and collections, and support drama plays were further carried out as leading role model projects in these areas. Artistic excellence was presented in such programs as 2017 national performing arts troupe show season, collective showcases of local operas nationwide, 2017 exhibition season of national art museum collections, national tour of Wenhua Award winner plays, national showcases of excellent puppet and shadow puppet shows, national showcases of outstanding plays put on small theatres, the 2nd traditional instrumental music showcase nationwide, the 8th China Peking opera arts festival, the 3rd China Opera Festival, the 4th China Western Symphony Week, the 5th China Poetry Festival, the celebration of the 110th anniversary of the birth of Pan Tianshou, and symposium to commemorate the 110th anniversary of China's drama theatre. More financial support was given to artistic creations, as National Arts Fund of China provided in total 738 million RMB as financial support to 1,001 arts programs in 2017.

By the end of the year, the number of art performance troupes[4] reached 15,752, an increase of 3,451 over the end of the previous year; that of the professionals reached 403,200 with the increase of 70,300. Of them, the art performance troupes managed by cultural departments at all levels reached 2,074, accounting for 13.2% of the total with 115,600 art employees, which is 28.7% of the total.

Table 1: General information of art troupes nationwide in 2007-2017

Year	Number of institutions (unit)	Number of employees (person)	Number of shows (ten thousand)	Number of domestic audience attendances (ten thousand)	Total income (ten thousand yuan)	
						#Shows' box office
2007	4512	220653	92.7	75895.6	829045	203757
2008	5114	208174	90.5	63186.8	933685	204842
2009	6139	184678	120.2	81715.9	1121559	288214
2010	6864	185413	137.1	88455.8	1239255	342696
2011	7055	226599	154.7	74585.1	1540263	526745
2012	7321	242047	135.0	82805.1	1968802	641480
2013	8180	260865	165.1	90064.3	2800266	820738
2014	8769	262887	173.9	91019.7	2264046	757028
2015	10787	301840	210.8	95799.0	2576483	939313
2016	12301	332920	230.6	118137.7	3112276	1308591
2017	15752	403197	293.8	124862.9	3421091	1478239

In 2017, all art troupes in China presented 2.9377 million performances, an increase of 27.4% over the previous year; the domestic audiences reached 1.29 billion, up by 5.7%; the number of performances for audience in rural areas was 1.8444 million, up by 21.7%, accounting for 62.8% of the total; the number of the rural audiences was 830 million, up by 33.8% over that of the previous year. The total turnover of the performing troupes was 34.21 billion yuan, an increase of 9.9% over the previous year; of them the income from performing arts was 14.782 billion yuan, up by 13.0%.

The amount of government-purchased public performances presented by art performance troupes affiliated to official cultural departments throughout the year was 160,700, with audiences of 132 million, up by 12.9% and 10.2% respectively. The number of the performances on traveling stage vans was 118,000, with audience attendances of 102 million.

By the end of the year, the venues of the performing arts amounted to 2,455, 170 more than those of the previous year, with 1,796,100 seats, increased by 6.3%. Among them, 1253 are state-owned. 71,000 performances were held in the state-owned venues throughout the year, up by 4.3% over the previous year; the audiences reached 27.13 million, an increase of 4.8%. The total turnover of art performances reached 692 million yuan, up by 25.0%.

By the end of 2017, there were 499 art museums affiliated to art administrations in China, 36 more than those of the previous year, with 4,576 employees, 21 less than the previous year. 6,757 exhibitions were presented by these museums year-round, attracting 37.24 million visitor attendances, up by 9.9% and 15% over those of the previous year respectively.

III. Public Cultural Service System

In 2017, further steps were taken to implement the Opinions on Accelerating the Building of A Modern Public Cultural Services System and China's basic public cultural service guideline standards. The Ministry also actively facilitated the promulgation of the law on public libraries of the People' s Republic of China, carried out inspections on the implementation of Law on Public Cultural Service Guarantee and key reform tasks mandated by the central government, and made sure that legislation and reform measures were translated into real results. Experience-sharing forum on public cultural service capacity building were organized to acknowledge best practices like "cloud cultural service" and "community cultural supermarket". Sample inspections on the capacities and caliber of township- and village-level cultural stations to urge them deal with insufficiencies and provide better services. Efforts were made to build more and better digital cultural stations, digital libraries and libraries on mobile devices. Private sectors were encouraged to provide public cultural services, and explorations were done to authorize pilot services providers of private nature.

(1) Public Libraries[5]

By the end of the year, there were in total 3,166 libraries nationwide, 13 more than the number of the previous year. The total number of employees of public libraries across China reached 57,567, 359 more than the number of the previous year. Among them, 6,502 owned senior professional titles, accounting for 11.3%, and 18,729 owned medium-level professional titles, accounting for 325%.

According to statistics at the end of 2017, the actual floor space used by public library buildings totaled 15.1527 million m^2, up by 6.4% over the end of the previous year. 909.53 million books[6] (among them 27.01 million were historical and ancient books) and 1026.27 million e-books[7] were collected in these libraries, up by 7.5% and 15.6% respectively. The number of seats in reading rooms was 1.0642 million, up by 7.9%, and that of computers was 221,000, up by 4.4%, and that of electronic reading terminals for readers was 144,300, up by 7.0%.

By the end of the 2017 the floor space of public libraries for each ten thousand persons was 109.0 m^2, an increase of 6 m^2 over the end of the previous year; the number of books per capita was 0.70, an increase of 0.05over the previous year; the money spent on books per capita was 1.70 yuan, an increase of 0.14 yuan over previous year.

Figure 2: Information of per capita resource of national public libraries in 2006-2017

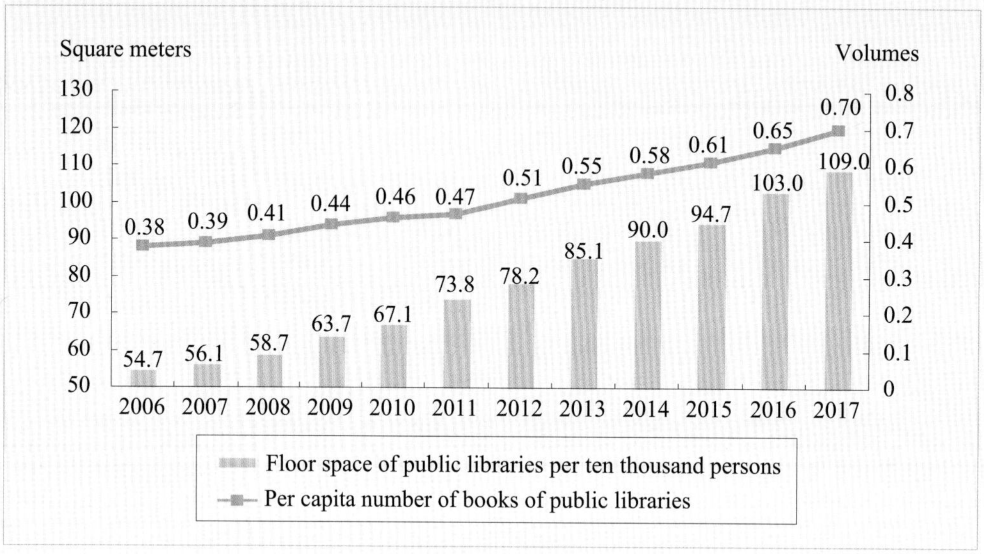

In 2017, library cards[8] issued by public public libraries across the country throughout the year total to 67.36 million, increased by 20.4%; the total flow of person-time[9] reached 744.5 million, a growth of 12.7%. The total circulation number of books, magazines, and documents loaned to readers reached 550.91 million, up by 0.7%; a total of 255.03 million person-times borrowed books, a growth of 2.5%. Various activities organized for readers total to 155,590, up by 11.1%; which attracted 88.57 million person-times, an increase of 24.1%.

Figure 3: Total flow of person-time and number of books lent out of national public libraries in 2006-2017

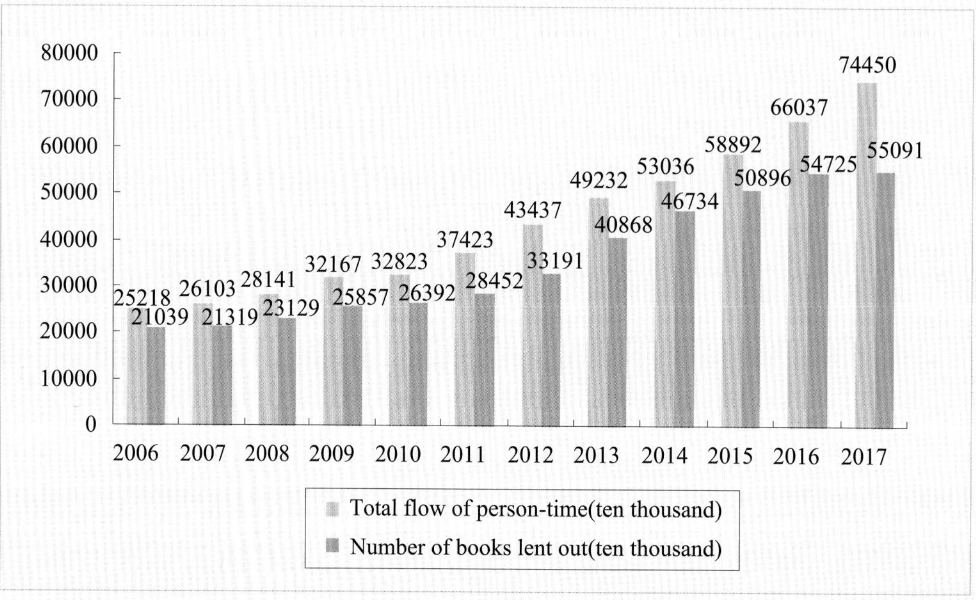

(2) Public and Community Cultural Institutions[10]

There was a total of 44,521 public and community cultural institutions across the country by the end of 2017, an increase of 24 since the previous year. Among these, township-level comprehensive cultural stations reached a total of 33,997, a decrease of 243. By the end of the year, the total employees of public and community cultural institutions nationwide reached 180,911 a decrease of 1,119 since the previous year. Staff with senior professional titles reached 6,171, accounting for 3.4%; and staffs with medium-grade professional titles reached 17,224, accounting for 9.5%.

By the end of the year, the actual floor space used by public and community institutions was 41,068,500 m^2, up by 209% since the previous year; among theme, the floor space used for offering public services was 29,774,600 m^2, up by 2.7%. By the end of the year, the area covered by cultural facilities for every ten thousand people reached 295.44 m^2, an increase of 6.80 m^2 since the previous year.

Figure 4: Area of structure of national cultural facilities of mass per ten thousand people in 2006-2017

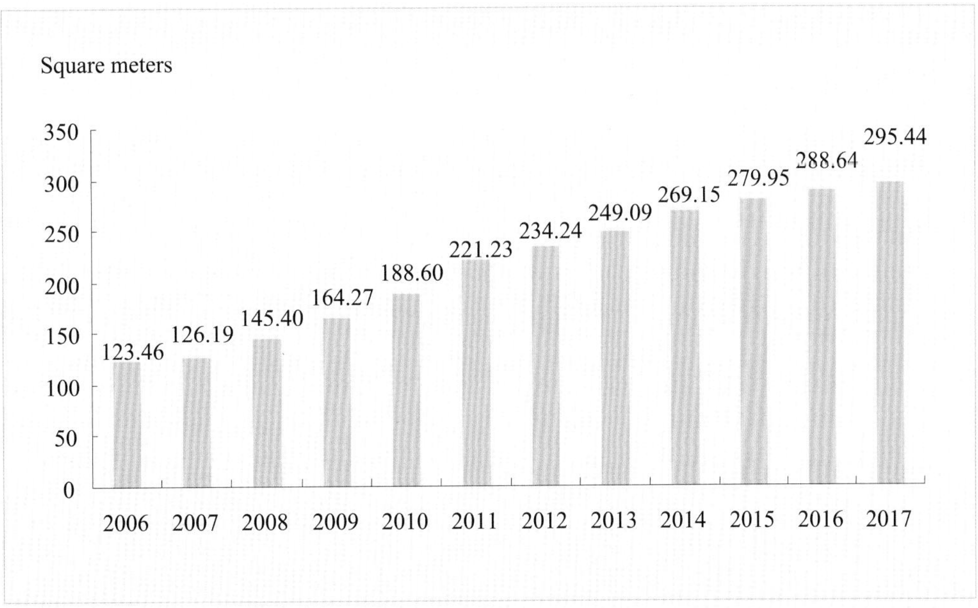

The number of activities[11] organized by nationwide public and community cultural institutions throughout the year reached 1,978,600, up by 7.6% since the previous year; total people served reached 639.51 million, up by 10.5%.

Table 2: Information of activities organized by nationwide public and community cultural institutions in 2017

	Gross		Increase over previous year (%)	
	Number of activity (ten thousand)	**Number of participants (ten thousand person-time)**	**Number of activity**	**Person-time of participants**
Aggregate of activities	**197.86**	**63951**	**7.6**	**10.5**
#Exhibition	15.41	10711	2.7	-0.7
Cultural activities	111.43	48183	4.6	13.8
Public lecture	3.44	562	1.8	7.7
Training class	67.59	4494	14.5	5.7

By the end of the year, public and community cultural institutions nationwide fostered a total of 8,241 cultural and arts organizations[12] under cultural centers, which presented 158,200 performances to a total audience of 82.29 million. The number of amateur cultural and arts organizations supported by cultural centers (stations) totaled to 416,700, and senior citizen's community colleges set up by cultural centers reached a total of 865.

IV. Cultural Market

In 2017, the Ministry continued to put focus on the source of issues as it encouraged culture-related businesses to improve services and image-building for the healthy, regulated and orderly growth of their trade and the market. 99 role model zones and 649 role model venues were acknowledged to implement the "sunshine entertainment action plan", which promoted of products and services of "sunshine entertainment" nature, and encouraged related consumptions. The Ministry published Notice on Guiding the Healthy Growth of Mini KTV Market, archiving 54,000 Mini KTVs nationwide. Measures for the Administration of Entertainment Venues was revised, and the MOU on Cooperation to Jointly Penalize Market Entities and Related Individuals with Significate Violation of the Laws or Credibility Damage was in the process of researching and crafting. Efforts were also made to implement various policies and supervise the standard measures of administrative review and approval, so that the “last mile” of policy implementation would be covered. The Ministry also furthered the reform of cultural market policing with a comprehensive approach, continued the capacity building of cultural market comprehensive policing professionals, implemented the 2017-2020 action plan for cultural market comprehensive policing capacity building in Central and Western China. In the random checks over the cultural market, 190 major cases were cracked open, 100 online entertainment businesses and 11,386 mobile streaming apps were reviewed, and 3,653 mobile apps for streaming online shows were taken off the market.

By the end of the year, business units[13] in the nationwide cultural market reached 257,400, an increase of 14700 over the number of the previous year. They employed about 1,733,700 people, 124,200 persons more than the previous year. There were 78,616 entertainment venues across the country, with 600,100 employees in total. Throughout the year, the sales of business units in the nationwide cultural market reached 54.687 billion yuan, with a gross profit of 13.069 billion yuan, a 1.5% and 3.9% increase respectively. The number of internet access services reached 143,434, with 440,900 employees. Their sales totaled 38.259 billion yuan, with a gross profit of 10.718 billion yuan, a decrease of 11.5% and 18.4% respectively.

V. Cultural Industries and Related Technology

The Ministry published Rules of the Government Cultural and Art Awards for Animations of China for nominating winners of the 3rd Animation Award of China. The Action Plan on “Belt and Road” International Animation Industry Cooperation were crafted to make animation a forerunner in China’s international cooperation across cultural industries. By the end of 2017, there were 730 cartoon and animation enterprises jointly approved by the Ministry of Culture, the Ministry of Finance and the State Administration of Taxation of China, among which 43 were identified as key enterprises.

Further efforts were made to promote the development and orderly management of cultural industry parks. Research were made to set up a benchmark system for building acceptance of such parks, as the name list of the first ten qualified National Role Model Parks for Cultural Industry was released and the special inspection on current National Role Model Parks for Cultural Industry was completed. By the end of the year, there were in total 1 National Cultural Industry Innovation Pilot Zone, 1 National Animation Industry Park, 10 National Role Model Parks for Cultural Industry, 10 National Pilot Parks for Cultural Industry and 335 National Cultural Industry Role Model Bases.

The list of 19 pilot cities (the second batch of the first phase) where the central government made special efforts to encourage culture-related consumption was released. The Ministry helped the cities clearly identify their working approach and take initiative in promoting culture-related products, and urged them to work fast with on-site supervision and special inspection measures. By the end of 2017, more than 300 million person times were engaged in the campaign across 45 pilot cities, leveraging more than 90 billion yuan worth of culture-related consumption. Efforts were made to encourage cultural institutions and museums to develop culture-related merchandise; with the support of special fund for cultural industries of the central budget, the total turnover of culture-related merchandise developed by154 pilot institutions has reached about 150 million yuan, 20% more than that of the previous year.

The Work Plan for Building Role Model Zones of Cooperation between Cultural and Financial Sectors was further harmonized, and Dongcheng District of Beijing and Ningbo city of Zhejiang Province were identified as the first candidates to become Role Model Zones of Cooperation between Cultural and Financial Sectors to strengthen linkages of the two sectors. After selection, the Ministry nominated 446 projects to be financed by special fund for cultural industries of the central budget, and obtained in total 588 million yuan as supportive capital. The Ministry also organized the applications for seats in the 4th batch of PPP role model projects, and facilitated the inclusion of 450 cultural infrastructure projects and 624 cultural tourism projects into the PPP comprehensive information platform of the Ministry of Finance, attracting in total 828.7 billion yuan as investment.

According to National Bureau of Statistics of China, the total revenue of 55,000 cultural and culture-related enterprises with annual revenue of 20 million yuan or more from their main business operations reached 9195 billion yuan, increased by 10.8% over that of the previous year, and 3.3 percentage points higher compared to the growth rate of the previous year. It was fair to say that these enterprises were growing at a steady and fast speed.

In 2017, the Ministry of Culture published the Cultural and Related Technology Innovation Plan of the Ministry of Culture for the 13th Five Year Plan Period, specifying the guiding principles, major tasks, key projects and insurance measures to carry out innovation on culture and related technology during the 13th Five Year Plan period. An improved system to subsidize projects in the national arts and related technology development plan added 336 new projects in its scheme in 2017, with the total supportive fund worth more than 680 million yuan. Further steps were taken to manage the national technology support plan and national cultural innovation project, and 12 projects were officially included in the latter. The reform on standardization of culture-related infrastructure and services was deepened, and the public was given unhindered access to the list of culture-related standards and national papers on said standardization. The project of building culture-related think tank was implemented to start 14 think tank projects. Under the Ministry's guidance, a league of provincial art academies and institutes across the country was established to better engage such institutions in think tank services. The first group of culture-related think tank contact points in enterprises were set up in five companies including Tencent, Baidu and Alibaba.

VI. Cultural Heritage Conservation

In 2017, the State Administration of Cultural Heritage (SACH) made tangible efforts in their work to preserve cultural heritage as they put into practice the instructions of General Secretary Xi Jinping for heritage work and implemented the Guiding Opinions on Advancing Heritage Work of the State Council of China. SACH crafted an overall plan on the preservation of the Great Wall, completed the preliminary version of provincial plans for preserving the Great Wall, and took stock of its special law enforcement tasks related to Great Wall. The key research projects themed "Archaeology of China" was carried out, more work was done to advocate the preservation of large-scale monuments, and the list of the 3rd batch of national archaeology sites and monument parks (12 in total) was released. Sach also drafted a five-year action plan to preserve and transmit revolutionary heritage, launched a project to commemorate the Long March, wrote the General Plan for Long-March Heritage Map, and advocated the projects to preserve revolutionary monuments and heritage sites in places such as Yan'an and southern Anhui. An evaluation of management of all World Heritage Sites in China was carried out, and commemorative activities for the 30th anniversary of the first inclusion of Chinese nominations in the World Heritage List. Gulangyu historic international settlement was put on the World Heritage List as a cultural site. So far, China has 52 sites inscribed to the List, ranking 2nd in the world. According to the first national census of movable cultural heritage accomplished in 2017, there were 108 million items/sets of movable cultural heritage properties and more than 11,000 heritage collection institutions in China. The rules and indexes to evaluate the operation and management of the level 1, 2 and 3 state-owned museums were revised and upgraded, the Opinions on Further Supporting the Development of Private Museums was published, and work to re-exam level 1 heritage items collected in state-owned museums and register collections in private museums was launched. The three-year action plan of "Internet plus Chinese Civilization" was carried out in a comprehensive way to advocate public sharing of heritage information.

By the end of the year, there were 9,931 cultural heritage institutions all over China, an increase of 977 from the previous year. Among these, 3,518 were for the preservation of cultural relics, accounting for 35.4%; and 4,721 were museums[14], accounting for 47.5%. By the end of the year, the number of employees by cultural heritage institutions reached 161,600, an increase of 10,100 compared to the end of the previous year. Among them, 9,221 were with senior professional

Figure 5: Information of national cultural relics agencies and employed persons in 2006-2017

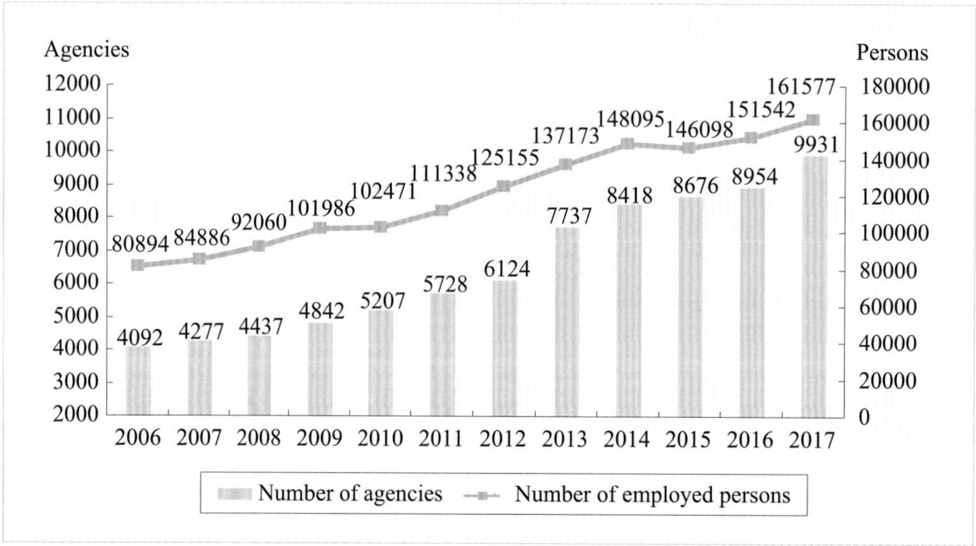

titles, accounting for 5.7%; and 20,136 were with medium-grade professional titles, accounting for 12.5%.

By the end of the year, there were 50.9632 million items of collections of cultural relics in the cultural heritage institutions, an increase of 6,404,400 since the end of the previous year, or up by 14.4%. Among these, the amount of collections in museums totaled to 39.3832 million, which accounted for 77.3% of the total; and for relics stores, a total of 7.3918 million, accounting for 14.5%.

In 2017, 26,045 exhibitions were displayed across the country, 1424 more than those of the previous year. Throughout the year, nationwide basic exhibitions[15] arranged by cultural heritage institutions reached 13,025, 823 more than that of the previous year; and temporary exhibitions[16] totaled 13,020, increased by 601; the number of visitor attendances increased to 1147.73 million, which was an increase of 13.3% over that of the previous year. Among these, 971.72 million visits were to museums, accounting for 84.7% of the total visits to cultural heritage institutions, up by 14.2%. Among the visitors, the number of minors was 289.09 million, up by 9.9%, accounting for 25.2% of all visitors.

Figure 6: Person-time of audiences and minors cultural relic agencies accepting in 2008-2017

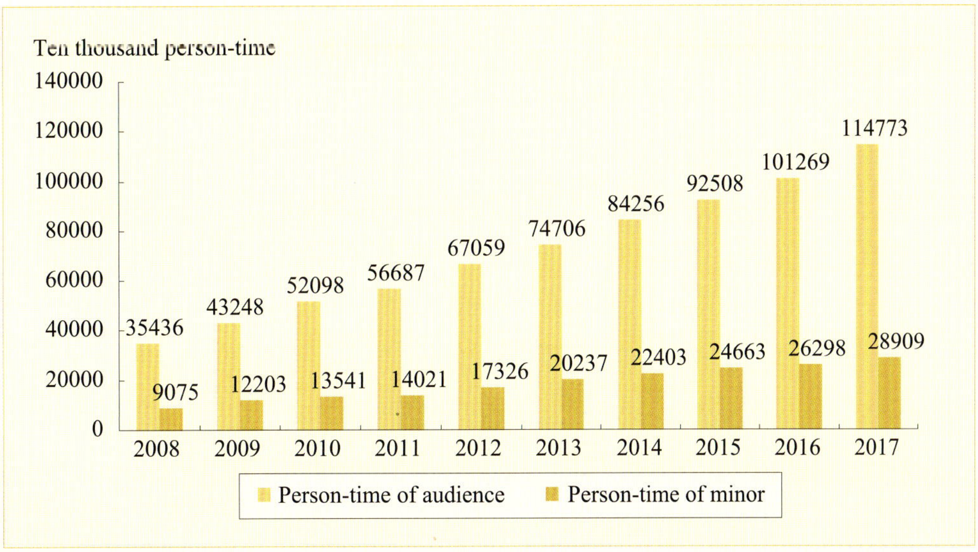

In 2017, the Ministry took active initiative to join all other related departments to draft a plan to revitalize traditional handicrafts as an overall guidance for the regeneration of traditional craftsmanship. Efforts were made to draft the national inventory for the first batch of traditional craftsmanship being revitalized, support the establishment of 10 traditional crafts work stations, upgrade the techniques and caliber of crafts, and help contribute to the targeted measures in China's poverty alleviation campaign. The Ministry supported 19 provinces, regions and cities to launch 28 dialogues with intangible cultural heritage (ICH) bearers, encouraged cooperation between bearers and design and research institutions, and facilitated the integration of traditional craftsmanship and modern life. Under the Ministry's guidance, 78 higher education institutions launched 2017 ICH bearer workshop programs focused on traditional craftmanship, hosting in total 196 sessions of training programs and workshops. The information management platform for such programs was initiated, a consulting experts's database was established, and teachers' capacity building classes and experience sharing forums were organized to advance the research of theories concerning ICH safeguarding and training conducted by colleges and universities. Workshops and training courses of traditional opera, folklore and ICH were hosted to enrich the ICH bearer workshop program.

The Ministry documented the practices of 839 state-level ICH bearers as a salvage action to save endangered ICH elements, and went through the review, check and acceptance procedures of 268 programs of the same nature in 2015. Further steps were taken to develop state-level ICH safeguarding and management facilities, and 335 million yuan from the central budget was allocated to support 46 state-level ICH management facilities to promote the integration of socio-economic development and ICH safeguarding and transmission.

Cultural and heritage days were celebrated in 2017, and more than 2,000 large and mid-sized ICH showcases were presented nationwide, attracting more than 100 million online and on-site audience attendances. The 6th Chengdu International ICH Festival was hosted, during which 579 showcases and activities were delivered to 326 local communities.

By the end of 2017, there were a total of 2,466 safeguarding units for intangible cultural heritage across the country, with 17,235 employees. Throughout the year in the country, these units held 50,178 showcases with 45.58 million visitor attendances, up by 19% and by 16.8% respectively. They hosted 15,133 folklore activities (up by 3.9%) with 62.11 million visitor attendances (up by 34.5%).

VII. International Cultural Exchange and Cultural Bonding with Hong Kong, Macao and Taiwan Regions

In 2017, the Ministry actively carried out intercultural programs based on various mechanisms, as demonstrated in its substantial contributions to China's eight high-level people-to-people dialogues with such countries as Russia, US and the EU. By the end of 2017, China has signed 157 cultural cooperation agreements and about 800 cultural executive programs with other countries, forming the foundation for an inter-government cultural exchange and cooperation network among China and most countries and regions across the world. The presence of Chinese culture at global stages were increasingly visible thanks to events and programs including China-US Cultural Forum, the 15th Asia Arts Festival, Cooperation Forum between East Asia City of Culture and European Capital of Culture, the first BRICS Cultural Festival, the 3rd China-CEEC Ministerial Forum on Cultural Cooperation, Insight of China, and Chinese/African Culture in Focus.

"Belt and Road" cultural exchange mechanism was built to cement the foundation for connectivity along the Belt and Road, and Silk Road leagues of international theaters, museums, art festivals, libraries and art museums were established or initiated. The Ministry also hosted the 4th Silk Road International Art Festival, the 3rd Maritime Silk Road International Art Festival and the 2nd Silk Road (Dunhuang) International Cultural Expo, attracting more participating countries and regions, presenting more shows and exhibits, and yielding more turnover than those of all previous sessions; encouraged all sectors to nominate key programs of Belt and Road cultural trade and investment with the aim to foster backbone cultural enterprises and flagship programs for stronger trade ties between China and Belt and Road countries in culture-related areas.

In 2017, Happy Chinese New Year Celebrations presented more than 2,000 festivities at 500 plus cities in over140 countries across the globe, making it one of the most visible external cultural brands of China that tells the stories of China through culture. Smooth progresses were made in the establishment of China Cultural Centers overseas. In 2017, with 5 newly launched China Cultural Centers in Athens, Hanoi, Sofia, Tel Aviv and Yangon respectively, the total number of

China Cultural Centers overseas reached 35.

Active efforts were made to implement the cultural bonding and cooperation executive programs between Chinese mainland and Hong Kong and Macau SARs and present brand cultural programs such as Root and Soul and Yihailiujin (literally, interflow across the golden sea of arts). Steady progresses were witnessed in cross-strait cultural ties, as demonstrated in such events as the cross-strait cultural and creative industries fair and cross-strait ICH month.

The year saw 3,054 international cultural exchange programs approved by government cultural departments with 63,961 participant attendances; 496 cultural bonding programs with Hong Kong and Macau, with 12,567 participant attendances, and 342 cultural bonding programs with Taiwan with 6,428 participant attendances.

VIII. Investment in Culture

In 2017, the central budget of China continued to subsidize local culture by implementing cultural projects, such as free access to museums, libraries, and cultural centers (stations), intangible cultural heritage safeguarding, digital cultural contents for public use and cultural infrastructure development at city-level. It provided special funding in total 4.933 billion yuan, down by 19.2% compared to that of the previous year.

Figure 7: Information of subvention of central authority to local cultural projects in 2006-2017

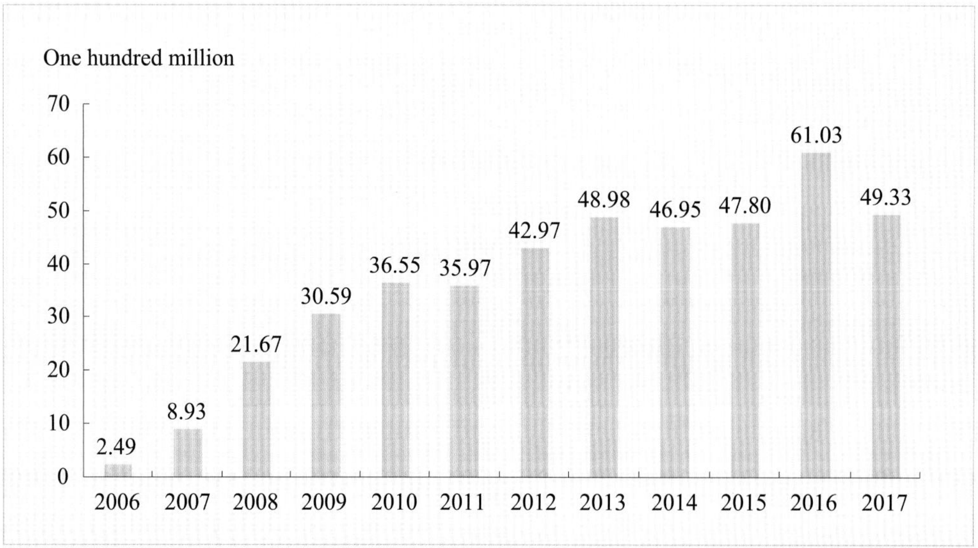

The total amount of cultural undertaking expenses[17] for the whole year was 85.580 billion yuan, an increase of 8.511 billion yuan over that of the previous year, up by 11%; as for the national cultural undertaking expenses per capita, the total was 61.57 yuan, an increase of 5.83 yuan over the previous year, up by 10.5%.

Figure 8: Information of cultural operating expenses per capita in 2006-2017

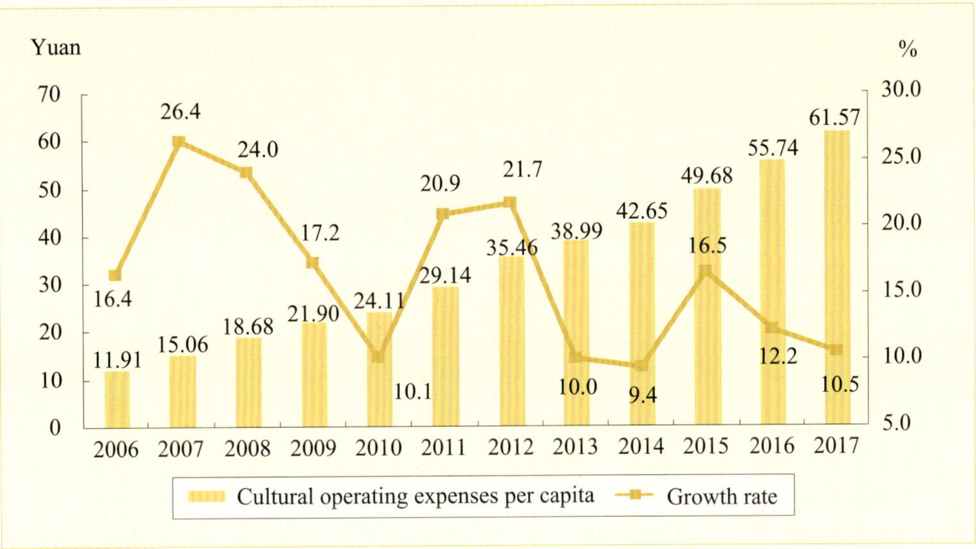

The national cultural undertaking expenses accounted for 0.42% of the country's total financial expenditure, 0.01 percentage points higher than that of the previous year.

Figure 9: Proportion of national cultural operating expense in financial expenditure

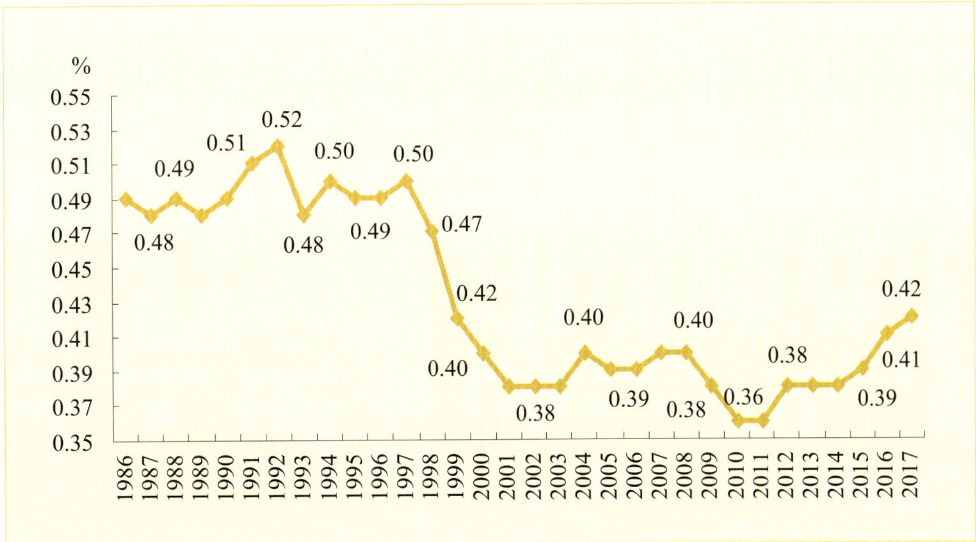

Regarding the national cultural undertaking expenses, that of cultural units above county level was 39.835 billion yuan, accounting for 46.5%, 1.6 percentage points lower than that of the previous year; that of cultural units of county level or below the level of county was 45745 billion yuan, accounting for 53.5%, up by 1.6 percentage points in the sense of its proportion. The cultural undertaking expenses of eastern region[18] reached 38.171 billion yuan, accounting for 44.6%, and its proportion increased by 1.3%; that of central region reached 21.330 billion yuan, accounting for 24.9%, its proportion decreased by 0.9%; and that of western region reached 23.070 billion yuan, accounting for 27%, its proportion decreased by 1.3%.

Table 3: Urban & Rural and Regional-based distribution of national cultural undertaking expenses

		In 1995	In 2000	In 2005	In 2010	In 2015	In 2016	In 2017
Aggregate (one hundred million yuan)	**Nationwide**	**33.39**	**63.16**	**133.82**	**323.06**	**682.97**	**770.69**	**855.80**
	# Above county level	24.44	46.33	98.12	206.65	352.84	371.00	398.35
	County level and below level of county	8.95	16.87	35.70	116.41	330.13	399.68	457.45
	# Eastern region	13.43	28.85	64.37	143.35	287.87	333.62	381.71
	Central region	9.54	15.05	30.58	78.65	164.27	184.80	213.30
	Western region	8.30	13.70	27.56	85.78	193.87	218.17	230.70
Proportion (%)	**Nationwide**	**100.0**	**100.0**	**100.0**	**100.0**	**100.0**	**100.0**	**100.0**
	# Above county level	73.2	73.4	73.3	64.0	51.7	48.1	46.5
	County level and below level of county	26.8	26.7	26.7	36.0	48.3	51.9	53.5
	# Eastern region	40.2	45.7	48.1	44.4	42.1	43.3	44.6
	Central region	28.6	23.8	22.9	24.3	24.1	24.0	24.9
	Western region	24.9	21.7	20.6	26.6	28.4	28.3	27.0

The amount of maintenance expenses of national cultural heritage[19] was 35.559 billion yuan, an increase of 4.789 billion yuan, up by 15.6% over that of the previous year; the maintenance expenses of national cultural heritage accounted for 0.17% of China's total financial expenditures, 0.01 percentage higher than that of the previous year.

According to the Ministry of Finance of China, of the national financial expenditure in 2017, the amount of expenditure for culture, sports and media[20] was 3367 billion yuan, up by 6.4% over that of the previous year and accounting for 1.66% of the total financial expenditure, and the proportion was down by 0.02 percentage points over that of the previous year.

Figure 10: Aggregate and growth rate of expenditure of national culture , sports and media in 2006-2017

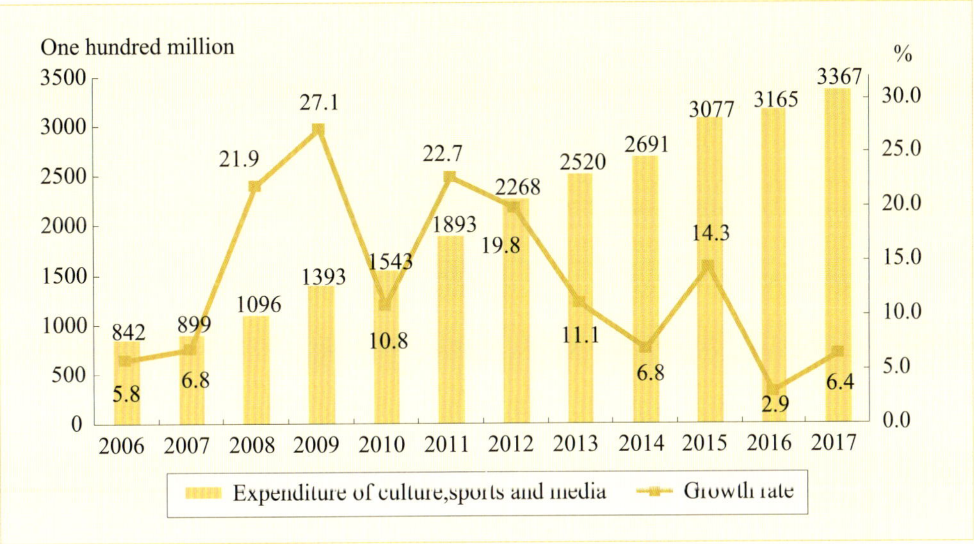

Notes:

[1] All the data of the communiqué are preliminary statistical data. HKSAR, MSAR, and Taiwan Province are not included in each data. Some of data are not compatible with the total of subentries due to rounding off.

[2] Cultural unit refers to cultural institutions that national cultural departments (including cultural system and cultural relic system) of all levels organize or implement industrial management, excluding cultural institutions organized or managed by the departments of all levels of press and publications, radio , film and television, etc. According to the current statistical system, the cultural

institutions (such as public libraries, cultural centers, cultural stations, museums, etc.) organized by cultural departments are brought into the statistical range. Regarding cultural institutions with industrial management, the private art performance troupes, cybercafé, and entertainment venues are brought into statistical range, while the mechanism of exchange of works of art, internet culture institution are not in the range.

[3] The employees refer to the people who work and receive working rewards in the institutions that cultural departments at all levels (including cultural systems and cultural relic systems) organize or implement industrial management. The statistical range is ditto with cultural institutions.

[4] The art performance troupes mean various professional artistic performance organizations which are organized by cultural institutions or to which the cultural institutions implement industrial management (with approval of cultural administration department and commercial performance license), and is engaged in such activities as performing arts.

[5] Public library refers to all kinds of institutions that are organized by cultural departments at all levels, and is open to public as well as providing popularization and education of science, culture, and other knowledge.

[6] The total collection of books in public libraries refers to the sum of audiovisual literature materials including bound volume, manual, manuscript, micro-reproduction, videotape, audio tape and CD of ancient books, books, periodicals and newspapers in catalogue. It does not include digital books.

[7] E-book refers to e-books both purchased and created by the collecting libraries individually or in collaboration with other institutions.

[8] The number of library cards issued refers to the number of library cards which are issued by public libraries and used at least once in that very year.

[9] The total flow of person-time of public library refers to the gross person-time of receiving the service of the libraries in that year, including borrowing books, consultation and participating in various readers' activities.

[10] The cultural institutions for mass public and communities refer to the places that cultural departments at all levels organize for mass cultural activities, mainly including cultural centers

(including comprehensive cultural center and mass art gallery) and cultural stations.

[11] The number of activities means the sum of the organizations of cultural literary and artistic activities, training classes, exhibitions, and public lectures.

[12] The literature and art groups refer to performance teams composed by the staff of this institution and that provide performances for the mass.

[13] The operating units of cultural markets refer to the agencies which are approved or filed by administrative departments of cultural markets and have relevant licenses and filing documents, and that engage in cultural management and services. In line with the current statistical systems, the statistical range of operating units of the cultural market only include private art performance troupes, entertainment venues, and business sites of internet access services.

[14] The museum refers to the non-profit and permanent social service institution which collects, preserves, and exhibits the witness of human activity and natural environment with intent of research, education, and appreciation, as well as being open to the public. It includes the units that carry out activities with proper names such as museums, memorial halls, science and technology museums, exhibition halls, etc.

[15] The permanent exhibition refers to the exhibition which is displayed in the pavilion, with fixed location and for an extended time.

[16] The temporary exhibition means the multi-formed exhibition which is set in the institution and designed by the pavilion.

[17] Cultural undertaking expense means aggregate of expenditures that the finance of all levels in the area invests to the organizer of cultural systems. It generally includes financial appropriation (excluding appropriations of capital construction costs) of cultural institutions such as art performance troupes, public libraries, cultural centers (stations), etc. and financial subsidies of enterprises subordinate to the Ministry of Culture. According to current statistical caliber, cultural operating expense does not include administrative operation expenditures of cultural administration and management departments at all levels.

[18] Eastern region includes Beijing, Tianjin, Liaoning Province, Shanghai, Jiangsu Province, Fujian Province, Shandong Province, and Guangdong Province; Central region includes Hebei

Province, Shanxi Province, Jilin Province, Heilongjiang Province, Anhui Province, Jiangxi Province, Henan Province, Hubei Province, Hunan Province and Hainan Province; Western region includes Inner Mongolia (autonomous region), Guangxi Province, Chongqing, Sichuan Province, Guizhou Province, Yunan Province, Tibet (autonomous region), Shannxi Province, Gansu Province, Qinghai Province, Ningxia (autonomous region), and Xinjiang (autonomous region).

[19] The maintenance expenses of national cultural heritage refer to the aggregate of expenditures that the finance departments at all levels in the area invest to the operation of cultural relics. It generally includes financial appropriation (excluding appropriation of capital construction) of operation institutions of cultural relic such as museum, protection and management agencies for cultural relics, etc. and financial subsidies of enterprises subordinate to cultural relic departments.

[20] The data of expenditure of culture, sports and media, which originates from the Ministry of Finance, is the investment of government at all levels in culture, cultural relics, sports, radio, film and television, and press and publications.